MEET

TRAVIS AND MOLLIE

Written by Barbara Gay   Illustrated by Libby Nickel
Second Edition
Copyright 2017 by Just Fun Books & Things.
4991 Manor Ridge Lane, San Diego CA 92130
All Rights Reserved. Printed in the United States of America.
No part of this publication may be reproduced or distributed in any form or by any means, or stored in a database or retrieval system, without the prior written permission of the publisher.
ISBN 978-692-87442-4   LCCN 2017902753

Travis is a lovable, furry, playful Goldendoodle pedigree.

He was moved from his birth home to his forever home when he was eight weeks old.

He was a gift to Grandpa on his 80th birthday!

Travis sleeps in Grandpa and Grandma's bedroom at night so they can be sure they can hear him if he is lonely and cries.

Travis was a very happy puppy. He had a big box full of toys, but he looked forward to the times he would get to go visit his cousins, Caesar and Cash. He also longed for another doggie friend to play with.

Grandpa and Grandma knew it would be best for them as well as Travis to get him a companion.

One day Grandma saw an article in the paper about a shelter nearby with Beagle puppies who needed homes. She and Grandpa visited the shelter with Travis, and a girl Beagle puppy was introduced to him. The puppy patted Travis with her paw, and they instantly became friends.

BEAGLES ARRIVE AT RANCHO COASTAL HUMANE SOCIETY

This pup is among the 35 Beagles taken to the Rancho Coastal Humane Society for adoption after being rescued from a home that could not care for them.

Grandma and Grandpa decided to adopt her and name her Mollie!

Now that Travis and Mollie are all grown up, they want to do everything together.

Sometimes they both sleep together in the same bed!

They always kiss each other when they wake up in the mornings.

They also kiss when they have been separated from each other for a while!

During the day, they spend a lot of time together relaxing and sleeping outside.

They like to rest in the sun on the lounge chairs outside.

Sometimes Grandpa and Grandma are upstairs in their recliners watching TV or reading.

When they are, Travis and Mollie like to lie down together at the top of the stairs to see if anyone is at the front door.

Travis likes to go to the front door when the doorbell rings to see who is there.

The window glass is not clear, but he tries to see out anyway!

Both dogs are always curious to know when Grandpa or Grandma are coming back after going out the front door.

Here they are anxiously waiting for Grandma to come back after going to get the mail.

Travis's favorite play activity is playing fetch with Grandpa with one of his many balls.

Travis expects Grandpa to play with him until he is too tired to continue!

Mollie's favorite play activity is playing fetch with Grandpa with a rope toy. She tries to keep up with Travis and Grandpa!

Here is Mollie with her favorite rope toy.

Travis likes to get attention by standing and walking on his hind legs!

He usually has a ball in his mouth, hoping Grandpa will play fetch with him again!

Mollie likes to get attention by acting like the entire backyard belongs to her.

She likes to sit on the edge of the firepit and survey her estate!

Both dogs love to go on any trip in the car. They are safely restrained with **dog seat belts** in the back seat.

Before she is buckled in, Mollie tries to hang over the barrier between the front and back seats.

They especially like to go on short trips and excursions to visit friends or relatives.

Here they are eating breakfast after a sleepover with their cousins Caesar and Cash.

Another favorite place for them to go is to get groomed. They get a bath, a haircut, their teeth brushed, and their nails trimmed. They do this once a month.

Travis and Mollie greeting Amanda, their groomer.

They also visit their veterinarian regularly for checkups and vaccinations.

Travis and Mollie are both very healthy. They stay that way because they eat good food and always have plenty of fresh, clean water.

Both Travis and Mollie took behavior training classes and are now very well trained.

This is Mollie at the door ringing the bell to go outside.

Both dogs expect a treat when Grandpa and Grandma go out and leave them behind alone.

They have learned to wait nicely when they are offered a treat!

Before bedtime, Mollie likes to rest on Grandma's lap on her recliner.

She usually falls asleep for a before-bedtime nap!

Travis also likes to relax next to Grandpa on his recliner at the end of the day.

He is now almost too big to fit on the recliner!

Travis and Mollie are very lucky dogs. They continue to live a happy life and are cared for, loved, and spoiled by their family. Their favorite activity is going to visit their cousins Caesar and Cash. They always try to get more play time and more treats! They still enjoy all of the other activities they had as puppies and young dogs.

JUST FUN
Books & Things

For Marcus, Chiara, Sonja, Leilani and their children.

Thanks to the following:
  Ray, David, and Astrid for their patience and help to the writer while working on this book.
  Jane for her help with proofreading and editing.
  Jeanette for her help in designing related products.
  All of the Humane Societies and other pet shelters who rescue, care for, and find good homes for all animals who need their help.

This book was inspired by the activities of Travis and Mollie--dogs who are owned, cared for, loved, and spoiled by the writer and her family. Travis was bred by Tropico Kennels in Palmdale, CA. Mollie was adopted from the Rancho Coastal Humane Society in San Diego, CA.
For information on other related books or products, contact JUST FUN Books & Things at justfun1936@gmail.com or by phone at (858) -342-3816.

www.ingramcontent.com/pod-product-compliance
Lightning Source LLC
LaVergne TN
LVHW072102070426
835508LV00002B/232